251 Excuses
Every Golfer Needs to Know!

The Ultimate Guide to Explaining Every Bad Shot
(A Funny Golf Gift)

Ricky Woods

Copyright © 2025 Ricky Woods

Published by: Bemberton Ltd

All rights reserved. No part of this book or any portion thereof may be reproduced in any form by any electronic or mechanical means, without permission in writing from the publisher, except for the use of brief quotes in a book review.

The publisher accepts no legal responsibility for any action taken by the reader, including but not limited to financial losses or damages, both directly or indirectly incurred as a result of the content in this book.

ISBN: 978-1-915833-83-9

Disclaimer: The information in this book is general and designed to be for information only. While every effort has been made to ensure it is wholly accurate and complete, it is for general information only. It is not intended, nor should it be taken as, professional advice. The author gives no warranties or undertakings whatsoever concerning the content. The reader accepts that the author is not responsible for any action, including but not limited to losses, both directly or indirectly incurred by the reader as a result of the content in this book.

View all our books at **bemberton.com**

CONTENTS

5   Introduction: Golf is Hard (But It's Never Your Fault)

9   The Weather Was Against Me

25   This Course is Unfair

41   My Equipment Let Me Down

61   My Body (and Mind) Weren't Ready Today

83   My Playing Partners Screwed Me Over

103   The Golf Gods Hate Me (and So Does Luck)

121   My Score Doesn't Reflect How I Played

135   How to Deliver the Perfect Excuse

149   Conclusion: Every Bad Shot is One Step Closer to a Good One... Right?

INTRODUCTION: GOLF IS HARD (BUT IT'S NEVER YOUR FAULT)

Ever watch a game of football and see the coach take the blame?

They step up to the mic after a loss and say, *"I didn't prepare the team well enough"* or *"The mistakes are on me."* The players follow suit, owning their errors and taking responsibility like professionals.

Other sports are the same. Miss a forehand in tennis — it's on you. Let in a goal in hockey — you take the blame.

That's what normal athletes do.

And then... there's golf.

In golf, personal accountability is about as rare as a hole-in-one. It's just not in the dictionary. When it takes you 104 strokes to limp through 18 holes, the only thing you *don't* blame is yourself.

It's the new clubs. It's the "crazy" wind. It's the Golf Gods, obviously.

And the longer you play, the better you get — *at excuses.*

A beginner might blame a light breeze and move on. A seasoned golfer? They'll act like a Category 5 hurricane showed up the moment their backswing started. Watch as they toss a tuft of grass in the air, squint into the sun, and shake their head like Mother Nature just filed a personal vendetta.

Why do we do it?

Maybe because we hear pros do the same thing—blaming lies, greens, fans, ghosts. Or maybe it's just easier than admitting what you already know deep down:

You're a terrible golfer.

But while we can't help you *play* like a pro (we're not miracle workers), we *can* help you *sound* like one when you butcher a shot.

This book arms you with an excuse for every disaster. We'd love to offer advice to actually improve your game—but honestly, there isn't enough paper in the world for the kind of help you need.

What we *can* do is help you blame with confidence. By the end of this book, you'll be spinning bad shots better than a dodgy used car salesman on commission.

So take notes. Study up. And prepare to take your excuse game to Rory McIlroy-level—one shank at a time.

THE WEATHER WAS AGAINST ME

1

Oh, today's going to be the day. You got the perfect amount of sleep last night, you were striping everything down the middle of the range, and the temperature is a perfect 70 degrees with not a breath of wind. Today's going to be the day... the perfect round of golf.

Fast-forward four hours and you're drowning your sorrows at the clubhouse bar, muttering the same words you do after every round:

"She did it again."

Mother Nature. The invisible giant. The devil in disguise. Her calendar revolves around your tee times. As soon as you tee it up, she throws a sandstorm (even though the forecast was 5 mph breeze). It's freezing cold on the front nine, then baking hot on the back (even though the temperature never really changed). She shifts the sun around just enough to screw with your reads (even though the clouds never showed up).

Oh, we have our reasons — cough excuses — for that 66 on the front nine. We've been here before. And to make matters worse, your mates won't shut up about it:

- **"That shot you hit in the water on 3?"**
  'Damn wind came out of nowhere.'

- **"That five-putt on 9?"**
  'The course rained on every hole but that one.'

- **"And the four-putt on 11?"**
  'Well, that one too. And 13.'

- **"You really camped out at the beach on 15."**
  'That bunker was wetter than Lake Michigan.'

- **"How'd you chunk your drive on 18?"**
  'Pollen got in my eyes.'

- **"Why'd you blade that wedge into the parking lot?"**
  'Tsunami-level gust. You didn't feel it?'

After hundreds of rounds of golf, we know the routine. We know who to blame. We've been here before, and we've come prepared.

We've got an excuse for every bad shot, every bad break, and every minor inconvenience that could possibly affect our game. We've memorized them. We've rehearsed them. Hell, we've even started to believe them.

Because let's face it — **we're far too good for it EVER to be our fault.**

Luckily, we've got a weather-related excuse for every kind of disaster:

"I can't feel the wind from the tee. It must really be blowing up there."

- **What It Really Means:** *Your ball went way offline, and you're hoping no one questions why.*

- **How to Sell It:** *Stand there nodding as if you're a meteorologist, then toss some grass in the air for dramatic effect and add a confused look on your face. Pros do this all the time.*

"There was mud on my ball."

- **When to Use It:** *Anytime your ball doesn't go where you planned — even on a dry course.*

- **How to Sell It:** *Wipe the ball like you're trying to polish a gem. Shake your head solemnly and mutter, "This course needs better drainage."*

"Water kept dripping down my face right before I hit."

- **Nice Try, But No One Believes You:** *You hit that same shank last week when it was bone dry.*

- **How to Sell It:** *Keep wiping your forehead like you're in a hurricane — even if it's just humid. Splash a little water on yourself post-round for dramatic effect.*

"The rain really ruined these greens."

- **What It Really Means:** *Your putts keep coming up a mile short, but you'd rather blame the weather than your lack of touch.*

- **How to Sell It:** *After every missed putt, crouch down, inspect the green, and scribble in your scorecard like you're writing a maintenance report.*

"The wind is everywhere today."

- **What It Really Means:** *That slice was happening no matter what, but at least now you can pretend it wasn't your fault.*

- **How to Sell It:** *Shake your head on every tee box. Mention "crosswinds." Ask, "Did you feel that?" at least five times.*

"It was so cold out there, my hands went numb."

- **Why This is Total BS:** *You were hooking your drives in July too.*

- **How to Sell It:** *Blow into your hands like you're in the Arctic — never mind the guy next to you in shorts.*

"I didn't account for the earth's rotation on that shot."

- **Nice Try, But No One Believes You:** *Even Bryson DeChambeau doesn't factor planetary movement on a 30-yard wedge. But sure, blame physics.*

"I couldn't grip the club because my hands were so sweaty."

- **When to Use It:** *Perfect in hot weather — especially when you're out of real excuses.*

- **How to Sell It:** *Wipe everything: hands, club, face, your buddy's glove — whatever makes it look like a swamp out there.*

"The sun was in my eyes."

- **When to Use It:** *Literally anytime the sun is out. Or not.*

- **How to Sell It:** *Squint dramatically and put your hand over your eyes like you're staring into an eclipse. Bonus points if you're wearing sunglasses while you do it.*

"This tee box is too slippery."

- **What It Really Means:** *That was a terrible swing, but somehow, the grass is to blame.*

- **How to Sell It:** *Scuff your foot like a horse and stare at the ground like it betrayed you.*

"That shadow threw my read off."

- **Nice Try, But No One Believes You:** *That putt never had a chance, but go ahead — blame the shade.*

"It's way too humid to play well."

- **Why This is Total BS:** *Humidity doesn't chunk a 9-iron. You do.*

- **How to Sell It:** *Wipe your forehead like you're melting, then casually mention — at least ten times — that you've gone through three gloves already. For maximum effect, let the club fly on your follow-through. "I can't grip my club. It's too humid out here." Your playing partners won't laugh because you said it... They'll laugh because your 9-iron is now floating in the pond.*

"I lost the ball in... something." *(Fog? Clouds? Darkness? Complete as necessary.)*

- **What It Really Means:** *That ball was gone the moment you hit it — but now you're blaming the elements.*

- **How to Sell It:** *Stare blankly into the distance, then mutter, "I think it just vanished." Drop a new ball confidently — like the rules support your delusion.*

"I can't complete my swing in waterproofs."

- **Nice Try, But No One Believes You:** *That jacket isn't the reason your approach shot skimmed its way into a different postcode — you managed that all by yourself.*

"The greens have dried out."

- **What It Really Means:** *You had zero feel, but the sun will take the blame.*

- **How to Sell It:** *After missing your putt for a double bogey, huff, roll the ball in disgust, and mutter something about the pace being "completely different" from five minutes ago.*

"I'm not used to playing above sea level."

- **What It Really Means:** *You completely misjudged your distance, but now you can sound scientific.*

- **How to Sell It**: *Pull out your rangefinder, shake it, then look skyward like the air is thinner than expected. Bonus points if you mutter, "This would've been perfect at sea level," and nobody knows what you're talking about — including you.*

"The rain made the ball heavier."

- **Why This is Total BS:** *It didn't. But thanks for playing.*

"The course is playing longer because of the cold."

- **What It Really Means:** *You're losing distance and refusing to admit you're aging.*

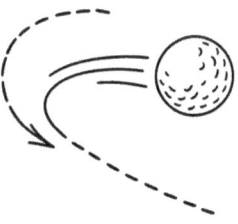

- **How to Sell It**: *Mention "air density" and stare at your 7-iron like it betrayed you.*

"I'm not built for cold weather."

- **When to Use It:** *Anytime you're wearing more layers than the Michelin Man.*

- **How to Sell It**: *Pull your beanie lower, complain between holes, and ask if anyone else's toes are numb. They aren't.*

"I wanted to keep the ball under this wind."

- **What It Really Means**: *You thinned it, but now it sounds like a strategy.*

- **How to Sell It**: *Nod like it was intentional and say, "Kept it low, just like I planned." Whether you meant to or not... you're showing off that low ball either way.*

"Even Tiger would shoot over 100 in this heat."

- **Why This is Total BS**: *Tiger would break 70 using rental clubs and a hangover.*

- **How to Sell It**: *Sweat through your shirt. Moan after each shot. Then ask for your fourth beer before the turn.*

"I can't see my ball with these damn glasses."

- **Why This is Total BS**: *It's not your eyewear — it's your swing.*

- **How to Sell It**: *Wipe them constantly, even if they're spotless. Ask if anyone saw where it went. They did. It's in the trees.*

"These fairways are waterlogged."

- **How to Sell It:** *Wipe your shoes dramatically after every shot like you've been hiking through a swamp. Maybe talk about trench foot.*

"It's so cold I couldn't feel my fingers... or the club... or my face."

- **Why This is Total BS:** *It's the middle of summer!*

"This pollen is messing with my concentration."

- **What It Really Means:** *Allergies are a convenient way to explain that triple bogey.*

- **How to Sell It**: *Sneeze like you mean it. Sniffle between holes. Cough on your scorecard if necessary.*

"The wind keeps blowing my putts off course."

- **Nice Try, But No One Believes You:** *That five mph breeze had nothing to do with your 36 putts on the front nine.*

- **How to Sell It:** *Back off your putts like you're at St. Andrews in a gale. Mutter about gusts. Walk around unbalanced for dramatic effect. Your friends will laugh... then quietly recommend a therapist.*

"That rainbow in the distance totally distracted me."

- **Why This is Total BS:** *Rainbows don't move. You do.*

- **How to Sell It***: Point it out like it's a hazard. Ignore the fact your shot went 40 yards left.*

"There's frost on these greens."

- **What It Really Means:** *That putt was always going to miss, but now the course is at fault.*

"The wind wasn't blowing on the range."

- **What It Really Means:** *You hit bad shots on the range too, but no one was watching.*

"I can't play with the sand this wet."

- **What It Really Means:** *You have no bunker game, wet or dry.*

"Nobody can play in this downpour."

- **What It Really Means:** *You're blaming three raindrops for a front nine full of snowmen.*

- **How to Sell It:** *Wipe your club like you're playing under Niagara Falls. Squint dramatically. Complain about visibility. Bonus points if you brought a snorkel — and pretend it's not weird.*

"The dew slowed that putt down."

- **Why This is Total BS:** *That was a hit-and-hope effort with zero touch.*

REAL WEATHER EXCUSES USED BY THE PROS

We've all made excuses — about the wind, the cold, the greens, the phase of the moon. It's practically part of the game. But surely the pros don't stoop to that level, right?

Oh, they do.

Here are a couple of *world-class* players who've blamed everything but themselves. Because when the stakes are high and the shot goes sideways... even the best start pointing fingers.

Sergio Garcia — 2002 U.S. Open

Sergio once blamed both the rain *and* the tournament draw for his second-round 74 in a torrential downpour.

> "If Tiger Woods had been out there, I think it would have been called."

Small problem: Tiger *was* out there earlier. He shot 68 — in the same conditions.

Bubba Watson — At Every Event

Bubba is known for shouting "Mud Ball!" any time something goes sideways.

Apparently, his shots are uniquely affected because they "don't spin as much."

Sure, Bubba. Most of us can't spin the ball at all. We're just hoping it stays somewhere on grass.

Crazy, But True

Temperature significantly affects how far a golf ball travels.

- **Cold air** is denser, which means more resistance and less distance.

- **Warm air** is less dense, giving you a little more carry.
- And at **higher elevations**, the ball flies even farther—because the air's so thin, even your mishits get a bit of help.

So, if you absolutely flush one on an 80-degree day in Colorado, you *might* carry it as far as Rory McIlroy's wedge on a cold morning in Alaska... if you're lucky.

Useless Golf Trivia

In 2020, four golfers set a Guinness World Record for playing a full round of golf in the coldest temperature ever recorded: 32 degrees below zero Fahrenheit (-35.5°C).

Yes, minus 32.

The round took place at Willow Creek Golf Course, where they bravely teed it up while most people wouldn't even leave the house.

The sad part? You'll see golfers in Florida throw on three jackets, a thermal hat, and complain of frostbite at 60°F (15.5°C). Meanwhile, these maniacs were out there in hoodies, chasing birdies in the Arctic.

THIS COURSE IS UNFAIR 2

Golf courses are like amusement parks — each one promises a thrilling ride of twists and turns... and none of them end the way you envision.

By the end of 18 holes, you're completely exhausted. Not necessarily because you hacked it around 100 times (but wrote down 90), but because you feel like you've been *systematically destroyed* by a course designed solely to ruin your day.

As you leave the grounds, you glare at the greenskeepers and maintenance staff. You know the look — the *"I know what you did"* look.

"Damn them. They got me again."

And you're right.

They stayed up all night, scheming, plotting, laughing over their evil blueprint to "get you."

- They grew the rough just thick enough to eat your ball alive.

- They filled the bunkers with sand — because they knew you'd be in there all day.

- They hired an elite construction team to throw hills, valleys, and lakes exactly where you tend to slice it.

- They squeezed the fairways in by 50 yards, shifted the tee boxes to aim at hazards, and tucked the pins into the most sadistic corners of the green.

"Oh, they're having a good laugh about it right now."

Strangely, though... it didn't seem to bother your playing partners. But that's only because the course wasn't *out to get them*. It's personal.

First Mother Nature. Now the golf course itself.

Fortunately, at the end of it all, you still feel satisfied — because deep down, you know you played the round of your life. It wasn't your fault you made a 10 on the 6th hole — *that green was like a skating rink.*

Nor was it your fault you racked up a snowman on the 9th — *who thought it was a good idea to build the Atlantic Ocean around the hole?*

Oh, we've got all the go-to lines you'll ever need. Lines so good, your playing partners will be convinced it wasn't you — it was the course that made you look like you've never swung a golf club in your life.

Ready to blame the course for everything? Here's how:

"These fairways are too narrow."

- **What It Really Means:** *You would have missed even if they were 100 yards wide.*

"The rough is too thick."

- **What It Really Means:** *"I miss every fairway so this is my main concern."*

- **How to Sell It:** *Get down on your knees and search for your ball like it's lost in a cornfield. Disclaimer: your partners can probably spot it from 20 yards away.*

"These pin positions are a joke."

- **Nice Try, But No One Believes You:** *The pin was in the same place for your playing partners, who just made par.*

"These greens are impossible."

- **What It Really Means**: *You have no touch whatsoever.*

- **How to Sell It**: *After every one of your 60 missed putts, look completely perplexed like the Golf Gods blew the ball off-course.*

"The tee markers are pointing in the wrong direction!"

- **What It Really Means:** *Your ball followed the tee markers just fine... you just weren't aiming properly.*

- **How to Sell It**: *Blame the maintenance team and accuse them of pranking you. Bonus points for threatening to report it to the superintendent.*

"These holes aren't regulation size."

- **Nice Try, But No One Believes You:** *You just can't make a putt.*

- **How to Sell It:** *Bring a tape measure and "prove" you're right — even though you're 100% wrong.*

"There's no sand in these bunkers."

- **What It Really Means:** *You skulled your shot 50 yards over the green... in perfect sand.*

"That water wasn't there the last time I played."

- **Nice Try, But No One Believes You:** *Golf courses don't just add lakes overnight. You're not at Disneyland.*

"There's no grass on these fairways."

- **What It Really Means:** *You chunked your shot and needed something to blame.*

"The grain is pointing the other way!"

- **What It Really Means:** *Your putt was terrible, but now you're blaming invisible grass physics.*

- **How to Sell It:** *Shake your head like you just solved a complex scientific mystery.*

"The rough swallowed my ball."

- **What It Really Means:** *You're already making excuses before you even hit your next shot.*

- **How to Sell It:** *On your next shot, take a massive baseball swing like you're trying to hit a home run — and hope for the best.*

"I don't play well on courses I haven't played before."

- **What It Really Means:** *You don't play well anywhere.*

- **How to Sell It:** *Stare at the course map like you're completely lost. Maybe even drive your cart in the wrong direction.*

"These yardage markers are completely wrong."

- **What It Really Means:** *The yardage markers are right — you just hit a bad shot...again.*

- **How to Sell It:** *Pace off the distance dramatically, then cheat the steps to "prove" your point.*

"Where did that creek come from?"

- **What It Really Means:** *You should've hit an iron, but you went full hero-mode with a driver.*

- **How to Sell It:** *Look at the course map like you're discovering a new river system.*

"Who decided to put a tree in the middle of a fairway?"

- **What It Really Means:** *You hit it into a tree that wasn't even in play. (Unless you're actually at Pebble Beach — then fair enough.)*

"These greens are too bumpy!"

- **What It Really Means:** *That tiny little hop had nothing to do with your putt missing by six feet.*

- **How to Sell It:** *Tap down imaginary ball marks like you're fixing potholes.*

"My ball is getting no roll on these fairways."

- **Why This is Total BS:** *Everyone's playing the same fairways. It's not the grass—it's your third shot on a par 4.*

"No one raked these bunkers."

- **What It Really Means:** *You're spending half your day at the beach—and not enjoying it.*

- **How to Sell It:** *Hack away, then show your partners how "unplayable" it is. Bonus points if you eventually just throw the ball out by hand.*

"These par-5s are way too long."

- **Why This is Total BS:** *What did you expect—mini-golf? If you want shorter holes, move up a tee. Or grab a putter and head for the windmill.*

"I can't get an even lie."

- **What It Really Means:** *The ball was half an inch above your feet, and you're acting like you're hiking Everest.*

- **How to Sell It:** *Lose your balance after every shot like you're walking on the moon. Bonus if you actually fall over.*

"There are pitch marks and divots all over this course."

- **What It Really Means:** *Those pitch marks didn't cause you to top it 50 yards—you managed that all by yourself.*

- **How to Sell It:** *Dramatically fix every invisible divot you can find—until you've used up all the sand in your cart and your playing partners have stopped watching.*

"This course doesn't suit my draw."

- **Nice Try, But No One Believes You:** *You don't have a draw. You have a slice—and not the kind you find at a pizza place.*

"These cups aren't cut properly."

- **What It Really Means:** *You're not missing the cup — you're missing reality.*

"Putting on these greens Is like putting on glass."

- **When to Use It:** *When you have no feel and treat the green like an ice rink — sending your ball halfway to the next hole.*

"These greens are way too small."

- **What It Really Means:** *You couldn't hit a green the size of the Grand Canyon.*

"There are so many trees it's like playing in a jungle."

- **What It Really Means:** *You wouldn't know if the fairway was tree-free — you've been in the woods since the first tee. Bring extra balls. Lots of them.*

"These fairways aren't properly mowed."

- **Why This is Total BS:** *You're complaining about grass while you're hacking it sideways from the woods.*

- **How to Sell It:** *Shake your head dramatically and pretend that ½-millimeter grass ruined your chance at breaking 90.*

"Where are the yardage markers?"

- **Why This is Total BS:** *You're nowhere near the fairway. In fact, you're so far offline even your GPS wants to call it quits.*

- **How to Sell It:** *Flail your arms and shout about distance like you're lost in the Amazon.*

"I haven't gotten a good lie all day."

- **What It Really Means:** *You haven't been anywhere near a fairway since your first tee shot.*

- **Why This is Total BS:** *If you spend the day in the trees, bushes, and bunkers... yeah, your lies are going to suck.*

"You can't get a good bounce on this course."

- **What It Really Means:** *You're mad that your terrible shots aren't being magically saved.*

"These bunkers are too deep."

- **What It Really Means:** *You're taking a snowman — and then some — because you can't get the ball up over a two-foot lip.*

- **How to Sell It:** *Squat down low in the bunker and yell, "I'm down here!" That's about when your playing partners will start googling local therapists.*

"The scorecard gave the wrong yardage."

- **What It Really Means:** *When in doubt, blame the paper. Not the three chunks and a shank you just played.*

- **How to Sell It:** *Pull out your rangefinder, shake it like it's broken, and start jotting random numbers into a notebook like you're disproving Einstein.*

"The greens aren't rewarding my good shots."

- **What It Really Means:** *You think you hit a good shot — but it wasn't.*

- **How to Sell It:** *Spin the club like Tiger Woods and shout, "Be the one!" as the ball veers sideways into a bunker.*

"The beverage cart ran out of beer."

- **What It Really Means:** *Congratulations — you finally found an excuse everyone can actually respect.*

- **How to Sell It:** *Call for emergency resupply. Loudly. Bonus points if you act like the empty cart ruined your back nine.*

REAL COURSE EXCUSES USED BY THE PROS

One thing you can always count on from the pros:
The tougher the course, the louder the complaints.

When it's a calm day at St. Andrews and guys are shooting 20-under, you won't hear a peep. But give them an Open at Carnoustie or Winged Foot — and suddenly you could fill three pages of excuses from a single round.

Some pros are smart enough to just mutter complaints to their caddies or spouses. Others? They want the whole world to know it wasn't them. It was the course.

Ian Poulter — 2013 Open Championship

Before he went to LIV, Ian Poulter was a regular on leaderboards — and occasionally on rant threads.

At the 2013 Open at Muirfield, Poulter took aim at the Royal and Ancient over what he called "ridiculous" pin positions after a windy, fast afternoon round.

He even went to Twitter to vent:

> *"Unfortunately, the guys this afternoon will struggle with a few pin positions. 8th hole is a joke. 18th needs a windmill and clown face."*

Small problem:
The 8th and 18th didn't seem to bother the 14 guys who shot in the 60s that day — including a few who birdied both holes.

Shane Lowry — 2024 Open Championship

After a third-round 77 derailed his chances at the 2024 Open, Shane Lowry didn't point the finger at his swing — he blamed the course setup.

Lowry said:

"You'd have to question why there weren't a couple of tees pulled forward. Today, honestly, 15 and 17... like 500 yards into that wind, it's, you know, yeah. They keep trying to make holes longer."

Also worth noting:
Billy Horschel teed off just after Lowry... and shot 69.

Crazy, But True

Want to create your own golf course? Start saving your money now (and have some patience).

- It can cost anywhere from **$3 million to $30 million** to build a course (*Source: American Society of Golf Course Architects*).

- And once you've built it, you'll need another **$500,000 a year** just to maintain it.

- From groundbreaking to final completion expect the whole thing to take **2 to 4 years**.

So yeah... keep buying those scratch-off tickets at the petrol station.

Or pick up some extra shifts at McDonald's. That should cover it. Eventually. Maybe.

Useless Golf Trivia

Don't let the name fool you: **Iceland** is more like *"Golf-Land."*

The tiny country has the highest number of golf courses per capita in the world—**one course for every 5,247 people**.

Scotland ranks second. **The United States** is tenth.

Then there's Greenland which is anything but green. They have exactly **two golf courses**, and the average summer temperature barely creeps above freezing.

(Bring a parka. And maybe a sled.)

MY EQUIPMENT LET ME DOWN 3

You're standing in the local golf store, scouring the racks like you're searching for The One.

What should I go with?
The Callaways look sharp. The Mizunos feel good. There's something about the face on those Pings that gets me excited.

And then you see them — like a beacon under a spotlight — the perfect set.
It's love at first sight.

After a few practice swings and a couple rolls with the putter, you're convinced:
This is the one that will change everything.

You take them home like prized possessions.
You brag to your friends.
You imagine the birdies and the trophies.

And then... reality kicks in.

Suddenly, those new clubs that were supposed to save your game are sending you into the woods on 6, drowning you in the pond on 9, and camping out in the bunker on 13.

You stare at them in disgust:

"*I gave you everything. And this is how you repay me?*"

And then there's the putter.
If your golf bag is your team, the putter is the wildcard.

Even when your irons somehow get you to the green, the putter is there to mess everything up — and take your soul with it.

There's no club in your bag that takes more abuse, more threats, or more profanity than your so-called "magic wand."

"I hit the putt perfectly... and you still missed!"

Of course, we can't possibly blame ourselves
for another disaster of a round.
Never.
It's always the equipment's fault.

When you miss 14 fairways and three-putt half the holes, don't look inward — **blame the clubs.**

And if you need a little help blaming them properly?
Here's a list of excuses you can borrow:

"My putter is cursed."

- **What It Really Means:** *You suck at putting.*

- **How to Sell It:** *Stare at your putter like Harry Potter hexed it. Start muttering, "You're in time-out, you useless piece of junk," while your partners quietly google "therapists near me."*

"I'm still adjusting to these new clubs."

- **Nice Try, But No One Believes You:** *It's been two years. They're not new anymore — they're vintage.*

- **How to Sell It:** *Keep them shiny. Wipe them down like you're polishing a Ferrari... right before topping another tee shot.*

"I need new irons."

- **What It Really Means:** *You need new excuses. These are already your eighth set in two years.*

"I'm not used to playing with a rental set."

- **When to Use It:** *After three holes and eight disasters.*

- **How to Sell It:** *Hold each club like it's an alien artifact. Sigh after every shot: "Man, if I had my own set..." (Repeat 18 times.)*

"These grips are too worn."

- **What It Really Means:** *You needed an excuse after your third shank in a row.*

- **How to Sell It:** *Let a club fly mid-swing like you're launching a javelin. Blame it on "bad grip traction."*

"My driver is bent."

- **What It Really Means:** *It's fine. You're just hitting every shot left. Tomorrow it will magically bend to the right.*

"My grooves are dirty. I can't get any spin on my shots."

- **What It Really Means:** *You're too lazy to clean them, and even if you did, you still wouldn't spin it.*

- **Why This Is Total BS:** *Even polished grooves wouldn't save your wedge game.*

"These clubs don't fit my swing."

- **What It Really Means:** *Something's not right...it's either your clubs or your swing. Survey says...it's your swing.*

"I forgot to bring my own tees."

- **Nice Try, But No One Believes You:** *It's a tee. It's literally one inch of plastic.*

"I'm not used to playing with these balls."

- **Why This Is Total BS:** *You couldn't break 100 with any ball.*

"These clubs are too small for me."

- **Why This Excuse Won't Fly:** *They fit you fine yesterday.*

- **How to Sell It:** *Bend your knees dramatically like you're using a toddler's clubs. Bonus points if you complain about back pain by hole 6.*

"This putter isn't straight."

- **What It Really Means:** *It's you. It's always been you.*

- **How to Sell It:** *Hold the putter up to your eye like a sniper sighting in. Miss again.*

"This driver's head is too big for me."

- **Why This Is Total BS:** *Last week, you said it was too small. Make up your mind.*

"My GPS gave me the wrong distance."

- **What It Really Means:** *The GPS was dead-on. Your swing wasn't even close.*

- **How to Sell It:** *Stare at the GPS like it just sent you breakup texts. Shake your head and mutter, "Technology's useless these days."*

"I forgot my rangefinder."

- **Why This is Total BS:** *Guys are shooting way better than you without a rangefinder. Yardage markers exist. (You just can't find them in the trees.)*

- **How to Sell It:** *Channel your inner Bryson DeChambeau. Pretend to calculate distances between bunkers, hills, sprinkler heads, and the clubhouse. Mutter complicated formulas under your breath:*
  "140 plus 120, divided by slope... carry the one... adjust for humidity..."
  You won't play like Bryson. But at least you'll sound like you belong in a physics exam.

"I hit the wrong club."

- **What It Really Means:** *You hit the right club—you just hit it wrong. Very wrong.*

- **How to Sell It:** *After the shot, shake your head, look at the club like it betrayed you, and mumble, "Should've gone with more club." You would've chunked that one too, but nobody needs to know.*

"I only have odd-numbered clubs."

- **Why This Excuse Won't Fly:** *Lots of players carry half sets and manage just fine.*

- **What It Really Means:** *Hitting a 6-iron instead of a 5 isn't why your ball is somewhere in the forest.*

"I forgot my golf glove."

- **What It Really Means:** *You're either broke, stubborn, or just desperate for a scapegoat.*

- **How to Sell It:** *After every shot, shake your hand like you just broke three fingers. Bonus points if you loudly blame a "massive blister" nobody can see.*

"I'm not used to playing with these shafts."

- **Nice Try, But No One Believes You:** *Your old shafts didn't save you either.*

"I can't play well without my hat."

- **Why This is Total BS:** *Plenty of legends won without a hat. You're not overheating — you're just overcomplicating.*

"The screws are loose in my driver."

- **What It Really Means:** *The screws in your driver are fine. It's the ones in your head that need tightening.*

- **How to Sell It:** *Jiggle the driver violently after every slice. Bonus points if you start "tightening" it with a tee like you're working in a pit crew.*

"My clubs aren't broken-in yet."

- **What It Really Means:** *You're hoping this excuse works until retirement. Spoiler: it won't.*

"My sand wedge doesn't have enough loft."

- **What It Really Means:** *You couldn't get out of a bunker even if you were handed a shovel.*

- **How to Sell It:** *Skull two bunker shots across the green, then point to the wedge and shake your head like it betrayed you.*

"These clubs just don't fit this course."

- **Why This is Total BS:** *You've played over 100 courses and still haven't found one that fits your clubs. Have you ever seen an ad that says, "Buy this Callaway set — perfect for only some courses"? No. Didn't think so.*

"These clubs always perform well in practice but not on the course."

- **Why This is Total BS:** *Breaking news: your clubs don't choke — you do.*

"I've never used this putter before."

- **What It Really Means:** *You're blaming the putter for those 33 putts on the front 9.*

- **How to Sell It:** *Walk around inspecting it like a rental car. Fidget with the grip, test different strokes — make it look like you just borrowed it from a stranger.*

"These clubs are too heavy."

- **What It Really Means:** *You're pushing every shot right and pretending it's the weight's fault.*

- **How to Sell It:** *Take a few labored practice swings, groan dramatically, and mutter, "Feels like swinging a sledgehammer."*

"I haven't played in these shoes before."

- **Why This Excuse Won't Fly:** *It's shoes. SHOES! What's next...you're going to blame your watch?*

- **How to Sell It:** *Walk around flapping your feet like a penguin. Bonus if you "accidentally" slip and blame your footwear.*

"I confused my nine-iron for my six."

- **What It Really Means:** *You're either dyslexic, drunk, or just a terrible golfer who hit the right club 100 yards short. (Probably option three... with a little bit of two sprinkled in.)*

"I usually play left-handed."

- **What It Really Means:** *You're a righty. You're just running out of excuses.*

"I was in between clubs there."

- **What It Really Means:** *You were in between bad options — and picked both.*

- **How to Sell It:** *Stand over the ball looking completely baffled. Flip clubs back and forth like you're trying to pick heads or tails. Then after you miss, confidently announce, "I was in between clubs." (Spoiler: whichever one you picked, it was the wrong one.)*

"I'm just testing this club out."

- **What It Really Means:** *You're on your 15th "test drive" and still think it's the club, not the driver behind it.*

- **How to Sell It:** *Take five practice swings, look very serious, then top it 20 yards. Repeat as necessary.*

"I think this club is broken."

- **What It Really Means:** *Your swing is broken, not the shaft.*

- **How to Sell It:** *Bang the club on the ground after each shot like you're checking it for cracks. (You're not fooling anyone.)*

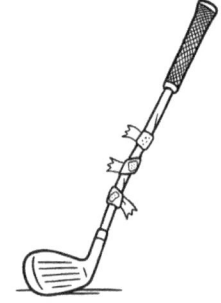

"There's a hole in my glove."

- **Why This is Total BS**: *A shiny new glove won't fix your slice either.*

"I used a sh*t ball on this hole."

- **When to Use It**: *Anytime you're terrified of losing a ball—so you grab the muddy ProStaff you found three holes ago.*

- **How to Sell It**: *When it inevitably sails into the water, shake your head and mutter, "Knew I shouldn't have trusted that ball." (Like it had a choice.)*

"My clubs are wet."

- **When to Use It**: *Anytime it's humid, misty, raining... or you just need a new excuse.*

"My golf bag is too heavy."

- **When to Use It**: *When you decided to walk 18 holes instead of riding a cart—and started regretting it immediately.*

- **How to Sell It**: *Carry your bag like you're dragging a grand piano uphill. Every time you put it down, collapse like you've just finished a marathon. Loudly blame the bag for your triple-bogey (on the second.)*

"I've only just started playing."

- **When to Use It:** *Every time you tee it up — whether it's your third round or your 300th.*

- **How to Sell It:** *Play exactly like you normally do. Bonus points if you use your putter off the tee or putt with your driver. Either way, the scorecard won't know the difference.*

REAL EQUIPMENT EXCUSES USED BY THE PROS

It's depressing hearing an announcer on TV casually say:

"*This is a 7-iron from 200 yards.*"

First thought: A 7-iron? 200 yards? *Is there plutonium lodged in those irons?*

But don't be fooled.
Those "super clubs" the pros use get just as much punishment as the ones you picked up at the flea market.

Sure, pros pay people to polish them, clean them, and wrap them in thousand-dollar headcovers... but the second a shot goes sideways, guess what gets blamed?

The clubs.
Not the swing.
Never the swing, and certainly never the player.

Bryson DeChambeau — 2024 Open

When Bryson talks, it's like decoding ancient Greek. You could spend hundreds of hours studying his "science of golf" — and still have no clue what he's saying.

At the 2024 Open, Bryson described how his equipment let him down:

> "I'm going to go figure it out. It's something equipment related. The golf ball is ... look, I'm not at 190 ball speed, so particularly when I'm hitting driver or 3-wood, those clubs are built for around that speed, that 190 ball speed, and my 3-wood around 180, so colder, firmer conditions the golf ball is not compressing as much. I felt like I was swinging it somewhat OK, just the ball wasn't coming off in that window that I normally see, so it was a weird day."

Translation: *Something, somewhere, somehow... was definitely not Bryson's fault.*

Bryson DeChambeau — 2025 Masters

Oh, we're not done with Bryson.

At the 2025 Masters, when his final-round collapse sent him tumbling down the leaderboard, he blamed (of course) a "lack of optimization."

Here's Bryson again:

> *"For some reason I'm just not fully optimized. I feel like I'm going to hit the heel and I try to pull across it and it just goes left. If I had good iron play this week, it would have been a different outcome... I kept hitting the heel. You're going to see some new equipment very soon, which hopefully will optimize my game to an even greater level. Super excited about it, actually."*

Translation: *New clubs = better scores. Maybe. Hopefully. Possibly. We'll see.*

Bernd Wiesberger — 2017 French Open

Not exactly a household name (especially after jumping to LIV), Bernd Wiesberger still made headlines for one of the **dumbest excuses** in recent memory.

At the 2017 French Open, after hooking a drive into the woods, Wiesberger claimed his driver had been "tampered with."

> *"I found out during the round that the settings on my Titleist driver had been changed by somebody. It happened to other players today too."*

According to Bernd, his caddie didn't do it. The security guards didn't see anything. So apparently, a rogue fan snuck into his bag, changed his driver settings... and no one noticed.

(For the record, Wiesberger shot a 69 — one of the best scores of the day. Still wasn't enough to stop the complaining.)

Crazy, But True

The rules of golf limit you to **14 clubs** in your bag. There's no specific combination — if you want to carry 14 putters, nobody will stop you.

(Some of us might actually play better.)

But someone forgot to tell Ian Woosnam's caddie at the 2001 Open Championship.

After birdieing the first hole and tying for the lead, Woosnam was told he had **15 clubs**—and was slapped with a **two-shot penalty**.

When told the news, Woosnam didn't exactly go full John McEnroe—but he wasn't a happy camper either. He grabbed the extra driver his caddie had added, tossed it into the trees, and muttered:

"I gave you one job, and this is what happens."

Of course, Woosnam could have just counted the clubs himself before the round.

But blame himself?
Come on.
Since when do pros ever do that?

Useless Golf Trivia

Remember when long putters were everywhere on Tour?

By 2015, long putters and belly putters were the golden ticket to trophies:

- Webb Simpson — U.S. Open
- Tim Clark and Matt Kuchar — Players Championship
- Keegan Bradley — PGA Championship

- Ernie Els — Open Championship
- Adam Scott — Masters

Naturally, once players started getting *too* good at putting, they banned it.

In 2016, anchoring a putter against your body was outlawed.

You can still use a long putter—but it can't touch your chest, your stomach, or anything else during the stroke.

(*Bonus excuse unlocked: "I would've made that if anchoring was still allowed."*)

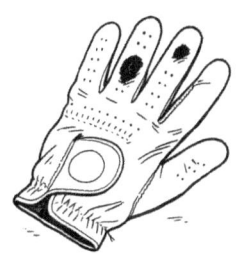

MY BODY (AND MIND) WEREN'T READY TODAY

4

Whether it's the last flushed shot you hit a week ago or the perfect warm-up you had this morning, the moment you step onto the first tee, you're as cocky as Tom Cruise in *Top Gun*.

Your body feels great. Your mind is razor sharp. Birdies are coming. Records will fall. Q-School is calling.

Fast-forward to the 18th, and you look more like Sylvester Stallone at the end of *Rocky I*.

Turns out, the only records you broke were:

- Most injuries claimed in a single round
- Most snowmen on a scorecard
- Most excuses delivered without blinking

In short: Your round usually goes something like this...

On the first hole, you tell your playing partners you feel better than ever. The course record is going down today.

By the second hole, a headache has magically appeared.
By the third, you're blaming a hangover from drinking too much... water.
By the fifth, you're dehydrated and furious there's *no* water.

Mid-round, the excuses move into full-body meltdown:
Your back's tight.
Your ankle's sore.
Your shoulder's out of joint.
Your pride left somewhere around hole six.

By the 18th, you just start freewheeling:

> *"I wasn't feeling it today."*
> *"I was just working on some stuff."*
> *"Next time I'll play for real... you'll see."*

Sure. We've heard it all before.

Two days later, you're back on the first tee, feeling amazing. And like clockwork — it's another crash landing.

This time, you've got fresh material. New excuses. Your body's suddenly gone through a lifetime of ailments... in 18 holes.

But the truth is, we never quite accept that maybe — just maybe — it's not the conditions, or the clubs, or the cosmic forces...

Maybe our golf game is just... infected.

Still, denial is more fun. So go ahead — try some of these wild excuses instead:

"I didn't drink enough water."

- **What It Really Means:** *Being properly hydrated would only make you more aware of how bad this round really is.*

- **How to Sell It:** *Walk around like you've just finished a desert ultra-marathon. Let your tongue hang out, pour water over your shirt and call it "sweat," then chug the cooler jug post-round like it's your favorite beer.*

"I didn't get any sleep last night."

- **Why This Excuse Won't Fly:** *You played fully rested last week... and shot the same score.*

- **How to Sell It:** *Yawn between shots. Groan mid-swing. Repeatedly tell your group, "I'm exhausted." Somehow, though, you'll be wide awake the second you hit the bar after 18.*

"I'm playing with a bad back."

- **What It Really Means:** *Your back's fine. Your game isn't.*

- **How to Sell It:** *After every shot, groan like you're 98. Bend down slowly. Stretch mid-fairway. Moan to your* group: *"I didn't have to play today, but I toughed it out."* They'll call you *"Grandpa."* Earn it.

"I didn't stretch enough before the round."

- **Nice Try, But No One Believes You:** *Stretching has never saved your scorecard.*

- **How to Sell It:** *After every bad shot, throw in a slow-motion lunge or neck roll. Act like you're prepping for the 100m final. Just don't pull a muscle pretending you didn't pull a muscle.*

"Something else is on my mind today."

- **What It Really Means:** *Yes — like that 8 on the last hole. Or the three water balls on 2. Or the tee shot on 6 that's currently being sniffed by a raccoon.*

- **How to Sell It:** *"Huh? What'd you say?" Look dazed. Stare off into the distance like you're trying to remember if you left the oven on.*

"I pulled my hamstring yesterday."

- **Why This Excuse Won't Fly:** *You don't use your hamstring to top a wedge. Also, you were on the couch all day yesterday. Did you tear it reaching for the remote?*

- **How to Sell It:** *Walk gingerly. Moan frequently. Go full soccer player and collapse if necessary. Just try not to laugh when you "limp" off the wrong leg.*

"I tweaked something on the range."

- **What It Really Means:** *You were planning your excuses before the round even started.*

- **How to Sell It:** *Choose a body part, commit, and exaggerate. Just don't forget which side of your body it's on — your playing partners will notice when you switch limp legs between holes.*

"My eyesight is bad."

- **What It Really Means:** *Your vision's fine — you just hit the ball 70 yards off target.*

- **How to Sell It:** *Squint like a cartoon pirate. Pull out*

binoculars on a 40-yard chip. Bonus if you blame it on your optometrist being on vacation.

"I was playing with a migraine."

- **When to Use It:** *After shooting 56 on the front and the back.*

- **How to Sell It:** *Whisper like you're in a library. Flinch at sunlight. Then immediately perk up when someone offers you a beer.*

"Nobody can concentrate with all this noise."

- **Why This is Total BS:** *Your partners are fine. You're just distracted by your own terrible game.*

- **How to Sell It:** *Give the maintenance guy a death stare. Shush your group like you're at Wimbledon. Then yell across the fairway like you're at a rock concert. Bonus points if a stranger tells you to shut up.*

"I have no confidence on these greens."

- **When to Use It:** *After your sixth three-putt.*

- **Why This Excuse Won't Fly:** *It's not confidence. It's your technique. Or lack thereof.*

"I'm playing sick."

- **Why This Excuse Won't Fly:** *You played worse last week fully healthy.*

- **How to Sell It:** *Sweat, sniffle, and fake-cough. Bonus points for a dramatic "I probably shouldn't have come out today." You probably shouldn't have.*

"I jammed my finger this morning."

- **Why This Won't Fly:** *It's a jammed finger. Not a career-ending injury.*

- **How to Sell It:** *Wrap it in tape like you're heading to the ER. Grimace after every putt.*

"I'm too anxious out there."

- **What It Really Means:** *You want this nightmare round to end... fast.*

- **How to Sell It:** *Channel Keegan Bradley. Fidget, twirl, pace, and talk non-stop. Make your partners wish you were anxious in silence.*

"I just have no motivation today."

- **Why This Excuse Won't Fly:** *You were fired up on the first tee. Then came hole two.*

- **How to Sell It:** *Stare at your phone. Sigh often. Let your club drag behind you like a toddler's teddy bear.*

"I have problems at home."

- **What It Really Means:** *You have problems with your backswing.*

"My body's sore from weightlifting."

- **Nice Try, But No One Believes You:** *Your physique suggests otherwise.*

"I'm too hard on myself."

- **Why This is Total BS:** *There's no "too hard" when your game's this soft.*

- **How to Sell It:** *Slam your putter. Self-scold like a toddler. If you break a club, that's commitment.*

"I'm too hungover."

- **What It Really Means:** *You had half a cider last night. Your buddy had 12 and is three-under.*

"I'm battling a lot of fatigue."

- **When to Use It:** *After you're out of breath walking to the cart.*

- **Why It Might Work:** *Hitting 112 shots does get tiring.*

"I'm overthinking my shots."

- **What It Really Means:** *You're not thinking at all — you're just inventing reasons to explain the chaos.*

- **How to Sell It:** *Back off your shot five times. Debate three clubs. Then shank it and mutter, "Knew it." Everyone else did too.*

"I think I have food poisoning."

- **Nice Try, But No One Believes You:** *You're just sick of your own game.*

- **How to Sell It:** *Rub your stomach. Pull a face. If you can fake gagging, you might get a sympathy Gatorade.*

"My shoulder!"

- **What It Really Means:** *My swing!*

- **How to Sell It:** *Wince, rotate dramatically, and clutch your shoulder after every miss. Let the pain magically disappear after your one good shot of the day.*

"I'm just too nervous."

- **Why This Excuse Won't Fly:** *You're playing for bragging rights and maybe a pint. Relax.*

- **How to Sell It:** *Deep breathing. Eye closing. Pretend you're at the Masters. You're not.*

"I rolled my ankle."

- **Nice Try, But No One Believes You:** *At least wrap it. Better yet, fake a boot. Bonus points if you sprint for the beer cart five minutes later.*

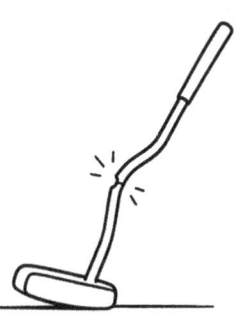

"I can't play when I'm hungry."

- **What It Really Means:** *You're craving pars but can't even score a bogey. The only thing you're feeding is your scorecard — with disasters.*

- **How to Sell It:** *Groan between holes. Rub your stomach like you've been fasting for 72 hours. When the snack cart rolls by, act personally insulted they're out of quinoa wraps — you're a vegetarian, remember?!*

"My elbow is bothering me."

- **When to Use It:** *When you've missed the last ten fairways.*

- **How to Sell It:** *Grimace like you've just thrown 90 pitches. Stretch theatrically. Maybe fake a medical time-out.*

"This girl (or guy) is on my mind."

- **Nice Try, But No One Believes You:** *You haven't dated since 2019.*

"I can't play when I'm angry."

- **Why This is Total BS:** *You can't play when you're calm, either.*

"I feel intimidated."

- **What It Really Means:** *You're playing with people who know*

what they're doing. You brought three sleeves of balls and a prayer.

"I had the last hole on my mind."

- **When to Use It:** *You had a snowman on 3. Now it's haunting you on 12.*

"I can't concentrate with people behind me."

- **What It Really Means:** *You can't concentrate with people anywhere.*

"My knee is in pain."

- **When to Use It:** *As soon as your game falls apart.*

- **How to Sell It:** *Develop a dramatic limp. Gasp when you bend down to tee up. Your partner might lend you their sympathy. Or their cane.*

"I was afraid of hitting the group in front of me."

- **When to Use It:** *After scuttling one just off the tee with a group barely visible on the horizon.*

- **Why This Excuse Won't Fly:** *They're 300 yards away. Your ball didn't make it past the forward tees. Relax — you're no threat to anyone but yourself.*

"All these numbers are playing with my mind."

- **Why This is Total BS:** *What numbers? No one asked you to do calculus. Just grip it and rip it.*

"I'm thinking too much during my swing."

- **What It Really Means:** *You're thinking. That's new.*

- **How to Sell It:** *Make a slow-mo backswing like you're Justin Rose being filmed in 4K. Everyone will be annoyed long before the club makes contact.*

"I woke up with a stiff neck."

- **What It Really Means:** *You got whiplash watching your own slice.*

- **How to Sell It:** *Icy Hot. Neck brace. Complain after every shot: "Where'd that ball go? I can't move my neck." Your partner replies, "In the water... again."*

"My doctor said I shouldn't even be playing."

- **What It Really Means:** *He was probably talking about your skill level.*

- **How to Sell It:** *Play the martyr. Moan about every joint. Use your putter as a walking stick. Someone might give you a hug. Or a lift home.*

"I'm not as young as I used to be."

- **When to Use It:** *When everyone outdrives you — including the retiree in the pink slacks.*

- **How to Sell It:** *Sip some prune juice. Moan like your knees are made of lego. Casually mention your cholesterol mid-round.*

"I have tendonitis in my right foot."

- **When to Use It:** *After you kick the cart out of frustration.*

"Sand got in my eyes."

- **When to Use It:** *After you chunk a bunker shot and move half the beach.*

- **How to Sell It:** *Rub your eye like you've been pepper-sprayed. Blame the wind. Or the rake.*

"I just had a tooth pulled."

- **Why This Excuse Won't Fly:** *Odd that your molar missed 14 fairways.*

"I already played 18 holes this morning."

- **Nice Try, But No One Believes You:** *Unless it was in the middle of the night or a video game, no one's buying it.*

- **How to Sell It:** *Talk about your "earlier round" like it was a triathlon. Maybe you mean the breakfast buffet?*

"I'm playing with too much adrenaline."

- **When to Use It:** *After nuking a wedge 50 yards long.*

- **How to Sell It:** *Be manic. Ramble about caffeine. Shake like you've had 8 Red Bulls. Bonus points for twitching.*

"I forgot my allergy medicine."

- **When to Use It:** *After chunking four shots in a row.*

- **How to Sell It:** *Rub your eyes red. Sneeze into your glove. Talk about pollen like it's radioactive.*

"I'm juiced up from working out."

- **When to Use It:** *When you sail one 30 yards over the green.*

- **How to Sell It:** *Brag about your gym PRs. Flex in the mirror. Act surprised when your pitching wedge goes 160 yards. "Guess I'm just too strong now..."*

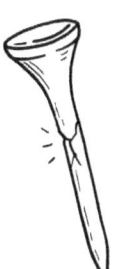

REAL BODY (AND MIND) EXCUSES USED BY THE PROS

We've all been there — watching a round of golf with a kid who looks up to the pros. Their favorite player starts hitting it sideways, and the kid turns to you:

"What's wrong with them today?"

You already know the drill. You look them in the eye and say, **"Wait for it... wait for it..."**

And right on cue, it happens. Grimaces. Stretching. A sudden limp. The full theatrical performance. Pros aren't just elite golfers — they've clearly had some drama training, too. And if it's going really sideways? Boom. WD. Withdrawn. Nothing saves face like pulling out with a "mystery injury."

Now sure, sometimes the pain is real. But let's be honest — other times, it's as exaggerated as a footballer clutching their shin after a gentle breeze.

And funny how that "injury" always disappears the moment they start playing well again...

Still, the excuses are legendary. Here are a few of the most gloriously overcooked examples from golf's elite.

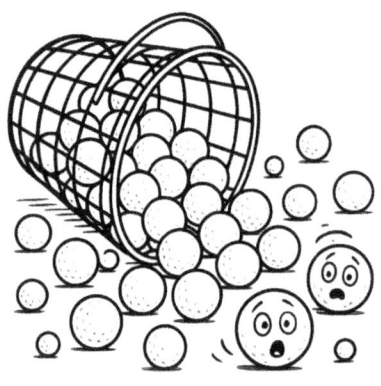

Rory McIlroy — 2013 Honda Classic

Rory was +7 in round two and clearly wasn't enjoying himself. The grimaces began. The body language dipped. Then, he hopped in a cart and left mid-round.

His excuse?

> "I've been suffering from a sore wisdom tooth. It was very painful this morning, and I was simply unable to concentrate. It was really bothering me and had begun to affect my playing partners."

Sorry, what? Affect your playing partners? Was he afraid it was contagious?

Not to mention — with the money these guys make, you'd think a quick shot of Novocaine wouldn't be too hard to arrange. Play high, sure — but at least you're playing.

James Hahn — On the 2023-24 PGA Schedule

Pro golfers live the dream:
Private jets. Luxury homes. Designer gear. Paychecks with more zeros than a binary code.

But James Hahn still took to Twitter to complain about... the travel.

> "Vegas to Japan to South Carolina to Bermuda to Mexico? For the viewers, it's a flick of the remote. For us, it's 20-hour travel days and tens of thousands of dollars of expenses."

We get it — jet lag is rough.
But Hahn earned less than $100K in prize money that season... while collecting $1.3 million as the PGA Tour's Player

Director and Treasurer. So about those "tens of thousands" of expenses, James...

Sounds like he saw the leaderboard and wanted to pre-load the excuses.

Crazy, But True

There's a story — classic Daly — that he once beat an amateur Tiger Woods in 1994 while absolutely plastered.

In an interview with Tucker Carlson, Daly laid it all out. The night before their round, he and his buddies got, in his words, "ridiculously drunk." Daly offered Tiger a drink. Tiger declined. Later that night, dressed to the nines, Tiger reminded Daly they had a fancy dinner to attend.

Daly, of course, had no idea.
"I got no shoes on, shirt untucked, s**t spilled all over me. Just drunk," he recalled. "I stumble into the bar, grab a guitar, play 'Knockin' on Heaven's Door,' get a standing ovation, and say, 'See you tomorrow.'"

Fast forward to the first tee at Sherwood Country Club. Daly's caddie hands him a Jack and Coke. Daly keeps the whiskey flowing. Tiger, stone sober and focused, is trying to ignore the chaos unfolding next to him.

"I grab my 3-iron and go on the tee," Daly said. "To make a long story short—I shoot 65, he shoots 71. He was shaking his head all day."

Moral of the story? Golf is hard. But it's apparently easier with a little bourbon.

Useless Golf Trivia

Jack Nicklaus once said:

"Golf is 90% mental and 10% physical."

That might explain why mental coaches have become as essential on tour as swing coaches.

According to *mentalgamecoach.com*, over 80% of professional golfers (men and women) work with a performance psychologist.

Some of the regulars include Rory McIlroy, Justin Thomas, Jordan Spieth and Keegan Bradley.

So if you're dreaming of a career in pro golf but your swing's tragic—don't worry. Perhaps you can become the one they cry to after making triple on a par 3.

MY PLAYING PARTNERS SCREWED ME OVER

5

Your alarm goes off at 6 a.m.

Today's the day. You're going to get there early, be first to the clubhouse, and play solo. No distractions. No delays. Just you and your clubs.

Fast forward to the Pro Shop. Turns out, 40 other guys had the same genius plan.

"Any chance I can play alone?"
"Afraid not — we'll slot you in with that threesome over there."

Translation: you've now got an audience.

"Ugh. I don't play well with people watching."
Yeah? Too bad. Get over it.

As you wait 30 minutes on the first tee and make awkward small talk with your new 'friends,' the excuses are already bubbling up. One guy is Mr. Rule Book — taking drop positions more seriously than the IRS. There go your 12 mulligans and six-foot wedges. Another guy talks non-stop. You know he'll be mid-anecdote during your backswing. And then there's Cigar Guy, fogging up the tee like it's Havana in July.

Over the next four hours, the chaos multiplies. You're rushed one hole, waiting 15 minutes the next. You forget your game plan. You blame your partners. You declare war on the group ahead of you.

By the time you hit the bar after the round, you've rewritten the entire story:
"If I'd played solo today, I'd have shot the round of my life."

Sure, champ. And if you'd been born with Phil Mickelson's short game, maybe you'd be on tour.

So now, to justify that trainwreck of a score, you explain it wasn't you — it was them. Here are some of the best excuses for blaming your playing partners for your collapse.

"Your shadow distracted me."

- **When to Use It:** *Early morning or late afternoon, when shadows stretch like skyscrapers.*

- **How to Sell It:** *Squint, shuffle, and act like you're lining up a putt on a solar eclipse. Miss, then glare at your partner like they've ruined your career.*

"Somebody yelled "Fore" in my backswing."

- **What It Really Means:** *Nobody said a thing. They yelled after your ball nearly hit a man two holes over.*

"That was a gimme. You should have given it to me."

- **When to Use It:** *Any putt inside 5 feet that you missed casually.*

- **How to Sell It:** *"If I'd taken it seriously, I'd have drained it." Sure, and if pigs could putt...*

"That lesson screwed me up."

- **What It Really Means:** *You needed that lesson. And five more.*

- **How to Sell It:** *"I was doing great before he changed my grip." (You weren't.)*

"The group behind us is rushing me."

- **What It Really Means:** *You've been spraying it all day and now they've caught up.*

- **How to Sell It:** *Keep looking over your shoulder like you're being chased. Complain loudly between chunks.*

"My boss keeps calling me."

- **What It Really Means:** *Your phone is silent, but your score needs a scapegoat.*

- **How to Sell It:** *Fake a grim conversation. Sigh heavily. "I've got to quit this job." Your partners agree — you should.*

"You were moving during my backswing."

- **What It Really Means:** *They adjusted their sunglasses. You hooked it into the pond.*

- **How to Sell It:** *Stop mid-swing. Sigh. Death stare. "Can you not do that again?"*

"The maintenance guy distracted me."

- **When to Use It:** *When there's a tractor anywhere on the course.*

- **How to Sell It:** *Act like you feared for his life. "He was right in my line." (He wasn't.)*

"I always play poorly when there are others watching me."

- **When to Use It:** *When you've got an audience — and no game.*

- **How to Sell It:** *Fidget. Wipe your face. Pull a Keegan Bradley. "I get nervous, okay?!"*

"You play too much by the rules."

- **When to Use It:** *When you're not allowed six mulligans and a practice swing with every shot.*

- **How to Sell It:** *Sigh like a martyr. "Fine. We'll play properly. Hope you're happy."*

"I'm distracted by my partner's outfit."

- **Why This Is Total BS:** *It's a golf shirt, not a disco ball.*

- **How to Sell It:** *Shield your eyes, wince dramatically, and mutter, "I can't focus with that thing in my periphery."*

"You keep talking during my swing."

- **What It Really Means:** *They cleared their throat. You duck-hooked it.*

- **How to Sell It:** *Glare. Pause. Pop in some earplugs.*

"You stepped on my line."

- **Why This is Total BS:** *They could have dug a channel to the hole and it still wouldn't have made a difference.*

- **How to Sell It:** *Stare at the green like it's sacred turf. Tap your putter in fake outrage. Announce your putt was "on track... until that." (It wasn't.)*

"You gave me the wrong yardage."

- **What It Really Means:** *They were right. You just flushed a wedge 30 yards short.*
  How to Sell It: *Pace it out like you're surveying a crime scene. "No way that was 125." Keep mumbling until they stop listening.*

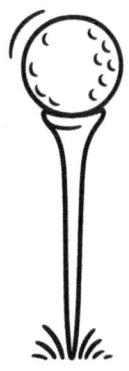

"Someone hit my ball."

- **When to Use It:** *On a busy day when your ball clearly sailed OB.*

- **How to Sell It:** *Insist you saw it land "right here!" Drive up and down a few times for effect. Then point at the next group: "That guy definitely hit it." Take a free drop with full conviction — repeat 11 more times.*

"My partner let me down."

- **When to Use It:** *Anytime you're losing in doubles — badly.*

- **Why This Is Total BS:** *Everyone knows you're the liability. But sure, blame your partner. Glare at them after every shot like they just sank your chances... and your self-respect.*

"Those guys in front of us ruined these greens."

- **When to Use It:** *After your sixth three-putt.*

- **How to Sell It:** *Sigh loudly, fix imaginary ball marks, and glare at the group ahead like they've vandalized the*

Mona Lisa. Meanwhile, your partners are draining putts just fine.

"Your marker was in my line."

- **Why This Is Total BS:** *You could've asked them to move it. Instead, you missed by a mile and now need something — anything — to blame.*

"These golfers are bringing me down to their level."

- **When to Use It:** *After you post a 96 and need to protect your ego.*

- **How to Sell It:** *Tell your mates later, "Normally I shoot in the 70s... but the group was all over the place. It rubbed off on me." Sure it did.*

"I hate when I have to wait."

- **Why This is Total BS:** *You play just as badly when it's wide open.*

- **How to Sell It:** *Sigh dramatically. Stretch like you've been stuck in traffic for three hours. Maybe even mutter, "I'm a rhythm player," like you're Rory. You're not.*

"That gum-chewing is distracting me."

- **Nice Try, But No One Believes You:** *Unless they're chewing like a cow, that's not what ruined your tempo.*

"You moved the cart in my backswing."

- **When to Use It:** *When you're last to hit and that shank was already locked in.*

"Those birds started chirping in my backswing."

- **Nice Try, But No One Believes You:** *Birds don't wait for your backswing. They've been chirping since dawn.*

- **How to Sell It:** *After the shot, look to the trees and hiss, "Seriously?" like the birds have some personal vendetta against you. Slice and repeat.*

"My partner keeps texting me."

- **What It Really Means:** *Your other half wants to know why this "quick round" is entering hour five. (Spoiler: It's because you're on stroke 112.)*

- **How to Sell It:** *Check your phone obsessively. Sigh like it's ruining your flow. "I just can't concentrate out here."*

Neither can your playing partners — watching you check WhatsApp every five minutes.

"Your cigar smoke is getting in my eyes."

- **What It Really Means:** *You just chunked another shot and need a smokescreen — literally.*

- **How to Sell It:** *Cough dramatically like you've walked through a bonfire. Rub your eyes like you've been pepper-sprayed. Glare at your partner like they just torched your scorecard.*

"You said the hole was that way."

- **Why This Excuse is Total BS:** *You hit it 100 yards offline, and now you're blaming someone else like they gave you bad directions to Narnia.*

- **How to Sell It:** *Point to three different fairways and complain about "confusing angles." Blame cigar smoke, shadows, and ancient signage. Bonus if you tee off in the wrong direction again.*

"The greenkeepers are trying to trick us up."

- **Why This is Total BS:** *The grounds crew didn't stay up all night plotting your downfall. They just mow grass.*

- **How to Sell It:** *Miss your putt, then crouch down like you're solving a quantum physics equation. Mutter things like "left edge, no — outside cup — wait...double breaker?" Then toss your arms up and say, "This is ridiculous." Your partners already know.*

"You put too much pressure on me."

- **When to Use It:** *Any time there's $5, a scorecard or bragging rights involved.*

- **What It Really Means:** *You're choking, but someone else must take the fall.*

"It's too busy out here to concentrate."

- **When to Use it:** *Perfect for a packed Saturday with five-hour rounds and groups on every tee.*

- **How to Sell It:** *Glance around in fake disbelief. Mutter about how you always shoot in the 60s on quiet weekdays (you don't). Roll your eyes like a teenager stuck in traffic.*

"It was my turn to hit."

- **When to Use It:** *When someone else swings at the same time as you.*

- **Why This Excuse Won't Fly:** *You were 100 yards away in the weeds. No one saw you, and honestly, no one cared.*

"I can't play with bad golfers."

- **When to Use It:** *Any time you're paired with players who are somehow even worse than you.*

- **How to Sell It:** *This is your chance to pretend you're Tiger in his prime. Strut like you're on the PGA Tour. Drop phrases like "tempo" and "release." Then chunk your next shot and remind everyone you're "working on something."*

"You gave me crummy balls."

- **What It Really Means:** *You lost all your good ones and are blaming someone else's hand-me-down Top Flite.*

"This round's taking too long."

- **What It Really Means:** *You're playing eight shots a hole and wondering why it's slow.*

- **How to Sell It:** *Keep checking your watch like you're late for a job interview. Yawn dramatically. Claim you're just trying to "keep pace."*

"You jinxed me."

- **When to Use It:** *Immediately after someone says "easy putt" and you miss by a mile.*

"I can't concentrate while music is playing."

- **Why This Excuse Won't Play:** *You can't concentrate in total silence either.*

"You hit my ball."

- **When to Use It:** *When your ball ends up in the bunker and you need a reason to take a drop.*

- **How to Sell It:** *Walk over solemnly, pick up the wrong ball, and say, "Wait... is this mine?" Insist someone else hit yours. Hope no one notices you're holding a Top Flite and not a Pro V1.*

"Your phone keeps going off during my backswing."

- **When to Use It:** *After you slice it, and your partner's phone buzzed five minutes earlier.*

- **How to Sell It:** *Flinch before your swing like you've been tasered. Shake your head and mutter, "Can't get into rhythm." Bonus points if you turn your own ringer off loudly like you're setting an example.*

"Mosquitos keep buzzing in my ears."

- **Why This is Total BS:** *It's called bug spray. Use it.*

"I thought you said it was a dogleg right."

- **When to Use It:** *After slicing it 60 yards into someone's backyard.*

REAL SLOW PLAY EXCUSES USED BY THE PROS

For most of us, a few minutes waiting in the fairway means time to check our phones, chat with our friends, or have a few sips of beer. The guys crank up Guns N' Roses while the ladies go old school Blondie.

The pros? Not so much.

Sure, John Daly might still throw back a cold one. And Spieth, Thomas, and Fowler can chat about anything. But for most tour players, waiting feels like a root canal. And every extra minute, the drill goes a little deeper.

Some players let it roll off—Scottie Scheffler probably just pictures his $50 million earnings and another bogey-free 65. But others? Let's just say there are a lot of Rory Sabbatinis out there—human ticking time bombs when it comes to slow play.

Nothing winds up a pro quite like the pace of play. And the moment their score climbs, the finger-pointing begins.

Tyrell Hatton — 2024 Masters

Tyrrell Hatton likes to play fast — think *Mario Andretti* in FootJoy spikes. But at the 2024 Masters, rounds one and two were crawling. Hatton wasn't having it.

> "Fine for them — they're not waiting on any shot that they hit. But for us, we stood in the fairway, we stood on the tee. It was really hard to get a rhythm. So it was disappointing that it took 32 holes for an official to go: 'Oh, we've put the group in front on the clock.'"

Translation: Blame the guys ahead. Blame the officials. Blame everyone except the guy swinging the club.

Meanwhile, *Matthieu Pavon,* in the same group, was tied for eighth. Didn't seem to hurt his rhythm.

Cameron Smith — 2024 Australian Open

Cam Smith started round two in second place... and finished in 16th. The reason? According to Smith, slow play — and possibly his playing partner, *Elvis Smylie.*

> "We got on the clock there and it didn't seem like we were playing that slow... but it felt like we were rushing."

When asked if Smylie was the reason they were timed, Smith did a world-class sidestep — basically implying yes, without saying yes.

Smylie, meanwhile, carded a casual 64.

His reply?

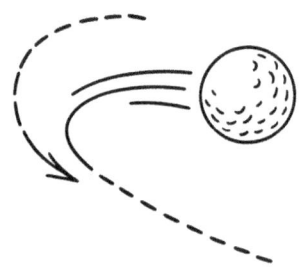

"It's a group thing, not an individual."

Translation: "Keep my name out of your post-round interviews."

Crazy, But True

Think you struggle when a couple of friends are watching?

At the 2018 Waste Management Open, a record **216,818** fans showed up.

20,000 of them crowded around the infamous 16th — aka "the party hole" — which feels less like a golf hole and more like the mosh pit at a Metallica concert.

So if you're blaming the pressure of a small crowd, maybe calm down.

Useless Golf Trivia

Wesley Bryan holds the record for the fastest round ever recorded.

At the 2017 BMW Championship, Bryan played 18 holes in **89 minutes**.

He was first off the tee, played solo, and *ran* between shots.

Why? Either to set the fastest round record — or because he really needed a bathroom. Either way, that's four holes for the rest of us.

THE GOLF GODS HATE ME (AND SO DOES LUCK)

6

There are certain people in life you really don't want to piss off:

- **Your spouse** — or you'll be sleeping on the couch, dinner courtesy of the McDonald's drive-thru.

- **Your boss** — unless you're planning to bag groceries until you're 60.

- **Your accountant** — forget their birthday, and Tax Day becomes a financial root canal.

But maybe the most important one, for golfers like us?

The Golf Gods.

Because once you've made them angry, it's over. Just ask *Phil Mickelson*. The USGA Golf Gods locked him in a karma bunker and threw away the key.

See, there are three sacred rules every golfer should live by. Unfortunately, you've broken all three — with enthusiasm.

1. **Don't get cocky.** Every time you step on the tee, you talk like you could beat Justin Thomas with your eyes closed.

2. **Don't cheat.** And yet, your foot wedge sees more action than your 3-wood.

3. **Never blame the Golf Gods.** And yet, after every hole, you're muttering "I always get bad breaks" or "They're out to get me."

Well guess what?

They are now.

Whining won't save you. Neither will superstition. But if you're going to dig yourself deeper with the Gods — and look a little less pathetic in front of your buddies — here's a list of divine excuses to lean on when luck leaves the building.

"The Golf Gods got me today."

- **What It Really Means:** *They get you every round.*

- **How to Sell It:** *Look to the sky after every disaster and whisper, "Why?" Cross yourself after putts. Refer to "them" like they're watching. (They are. And they're laughing.)*

"This hole hates me."

- **Why This is Total BS:** *You've played 180 holes and haven't found one that likes you. And why would they? You treat them all like garbage — shanking balls into their darkest corners.*

"My ball always lands in a divot."

- **What It Really Means:** *Either you're wildly exaggerating, or you think a dirt patch in the trees is "fairway."*

- **How to Sell It:** *Shake your head like you've just opened a massive vet bill. Then swing like you're chopping wood and blame the turf for the 20-yard dribbler.*

"That would have been perfect if not for that sprinkler head."

- **When to Use It:** *Any time your ball hits anything near the green.*

"I'm always getting bad breaks."

- **Nice Try, But No One Believes You:** *To get a bad break, you need to hit a half-decent shot. Yours are headed so far right they need passports.*

"My ball always plugs in these bunkers."

- **When to Use It:** *Every time you visit your second home — the sand trap.*

- **How to Sell It:** *Step on the ball when no one's watching. Act shocked. "Look at this lie!" Doesn't matter — you weren't getting out anyway.*

"The wind only blows when I hit."

- **Nice Try, But No One Believes You:** *You're playing in a light breeze, not a cyclone. The odds of the wind picking up only during your 104 shots? Astronomical. The only thing blowing is your scorecard.*

"Every putt is a lip out."

- **What It Really Means:** *You're smashing tap-ins like a Happy Gilmore drive and wondering why they won't drop.*

- **How to Sell It:** *React like your lottery ticket missed by one number. Drop to your knees. Look skyward. Curse the cup.*

"My drives always bounce off the fairway into the rough."

- **What It Really Means:** *You barely clipped the fairway on the way to disaster.*

- **How to Sell It:** *Stare at the ball in the rough like it betrayed you. Mutter something about "perfect bounce... wasted." Then hook the next one into the trees and blame karma.*

"The putt did the opposite of what it was supposed to do."

- **What It Really Means:** *It did exactly what gravity told it to. You're just bad at reading greens. And basic physics.*

"My perfect shot hit something and went out of bounds."

- **What It Really Means:** *It was heading out anyway, but now you have a scapegoat.*

- **How to Sell It:** *Point to a fencepost, a squirrel, or a mystery branch no one saw. "Right off that! Did you see it?" They didn't. And neither did you.*

"This golf ball always gives me bad luck."

- **Why This Excuse Won't Fly:** *It's a ball, not a voodoo doll.*

- **How to Sell It:** *Hold it up like it's cursed. Toss it in a lake like it wronged your family. Announce you're "switching brands." As if that's the issue.*

"I couldn't find my lucky shirt."

- **What It Really Means:** *Your laundry day is now your downfall.*

- **How to Sell It:** *Mention your last great round in that shirt. Then point at your current outfit like it's to blame. "I knew this polo was cursed."*

"My driver hates me."

- **Nice Try, But No One Believes You:** *Not sure your driver ever actually liked you.*

"This course is cursed."

- **What It Really Means:** *You're racking up doubles while your partners are cruising. Somehow, the curse only affects you.*

"My ball was half in the fairway and half in the rough."

- **What It Really Means:** *Congrats — this is the closest you've been to a fairway all day.*

- **How To Sell It:** *Stand over your ball and groan like you've just discovered a crime scene. Nudge it with your foot while nobody's looking. "Total bad break."*

"The ball was above my feet and didn't hook?!"

- **What It Really Means:** *You needed solid contact for that to happen. You... didn't.*

"These clubs hate me."

- **Why This Excuse Won't Fly:** *Your clubs, ball, bag, and shoes all want you gone. You're the common denominator.*

"I always play poorly with this guy."

- **When to Use It:** *When you're getting thumped by your usual partner (again).*

- **How to Sell It:** *Talk up their skills like they're on the Tour. "I'm cursed around this guy!" You are. It's called inferiority.*

"I hit the flagstick, and it flew off the green."

- **What It Really Means:** *You hit a rocket that deserved to be out of bounds. The flag saved you.*

"Luck has not been on my side today."

- **Nice Try, But No One Believes You:** *You're not unlucky. You're just... you. And that's the problem.*

"I never get a good lie."

- **What It Really Means:** *Stop hitting it 40 yards offline and you might find one.*

"That putt was supposed to go in."

- **What It Really Means:** *It wasn't.*

- **How to Sell It:** *Start fist-pumping before it drops, then collapse dramatically when it lips out. Blame the wind. Or ghosts.*

"The Golf Gods are conspiring against me."

- **Nice Try, But No One Believes You:** *They're not plotting. They're just watching you implode and taking notes.*

"I lost my lucky coin."

- **Why This is Total BS:** *The only thing your coin ever brought you was a triple bogey and some pocket fluff.*

"I got a bad bounce off that cart path."

- **What It Really Means:** *Your shot was already trash. The cart path just gave it a bit more flair.*

"My ball always bounces away from the hole."

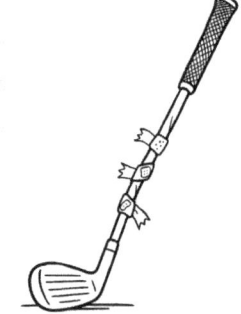

- **What It Really Means:** *You hit it like a drunken kangaroo. The bounce was mercy.*

"I never get this unlucky during a round."

- **What It Really Means:** *This is your normal.*

"The Golf Gods stopped that ball short."

- **When to Use It:** *Any time your putt dies just before the cup.*

- **How to Sell It:** *Drop to your knees. Blow on the ball. Yell "Go home!" like you're auditioning for Happy Gilmore 2. Bonus points if your partners quietly start Googling therapists.*

"My ball would have gone in if not for that rock."

- **What It Really Means:** *That rock saved you from a 40-footer off the green.*

"I always risk and never get rewarded."

- **Why This is Total BS:** *You've got no business playing "hero golf" when you're barely breaking 100.*

- **How to Sell It:** *Go for the green in two, chunk it into the water, and mumble, "I knew I should've laid up." Then blame the Golf Gods for punishing your bravery.*

"My ball is doing whatever it wants."

- **What It Really Means:** *No — it's doing exactly what your swing told it to.*

"That lady behind us put a hex on me."

- **Nice Try, But No One Believes You:** *Unless she's wearing a cloak and flying a broom, your round is on you.*

- **How to Sell It:** *Glance over your shoulder after every bad shot like she's conjuring something. Whisper about "the curse." Watch your partners quietly edge away.*

"These yips came out of nowhere."

- **When to Use It:** *After duffing every chip and putting like you've got the hiccups.*

- **How to Sell It:** *Shake your hands like they're possessed. Blame your wedge. Or your childhood. Just don't let anyone remind you this is your 10th straight round like this.*

"This course only plays hard when I play."

- **Nice Try, But No One Believes You:** *Your partners just birdied the same hole you quadrupled.*

- **How to Sell It:** *Say "They must've moved the pins since yesterday." Say it confidently. Then top your drive and pretend you didn't.*

"Golf is just unfair."

- **When to Use It:** *When nothing else is left in the excuse tank.*

- **How to Sell It:** *Glare at the sky like it owes you something. Complain about the bounce, the lip-out, the wind, the grass, your horoscope...*

"That tree came out of nowhere."

- **Why This is Total BS:** *It's been standing there since the Eisenhower administration.*

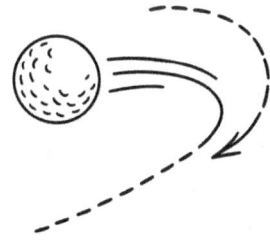

- **How to Sell It:** *Stare at the trunk like it stepped into your shot. "It wasn't there yesterday," you claim. No one believes you.*

"I skipped Church and God is getting even with me."

- **When to Use It:** *Sunday morning + awful round = divine punishment.*

- **How to Sell It:** *Shake your head and say, "I knew I should've gone to mass." Say it with a sigh, like Morgan Freeman's narrating your downfall.*

REAL BAD BREAK EXCUSES USED BY THE PROS

Arnold Palmer once said, *"The more you practice, the luckier you get."*

Clearly, Mr. Palmer never met the average weekend warrior. That advice doesn't apply.

But it does apply to the pros. If you hit golf balls 12 hours a day for 30 years, you're going to get a few lucky breaks. And they do. Constantly. Which is why they get spoiled—and start believing the Golf Gods are personally rooting for them.

They'll hit 71 great shots, but when the 72nd one takes a bad bounce off a sprinkler head or lips out, they lose it. That one misfortune? Suddenly, it's a tragedy.

And we get it. As amateurs, we can't *buy* a good break. So when we turn on the TV and watch millionaires complain after one bad bounce, it's hard not to roll our eyes.

Max Homa — 2023 Sentry Championship

Homa's strong second round went sideways on 18 when his approach hit a sprinkler head, bounced backward, and landed in a bush. He made bogey and carded a 70.

He avoided reporters that day — clearly not in the mood. But after bouncing back with a 62 the next day, he opened up:

> "Someone maybe in a thousand years will find a Titleist with a black marking on it, and hopefully they'll send it to the Bad Break Hall of Fame."

Sergio Garcia — 2007 Open Championship

If there's a *Golf Excuse Hall of Fame*, Sergio's already been inducted. In '07, he missed a putt to win on the 72nd hole and later lost in a playoff to Padraig Harrington. Cue the violin:

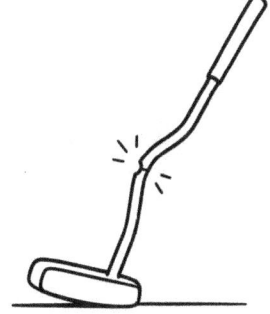

> *"I hit a perfect putt. I still believe that. Perfect. Halfway to the hole I knew it was going in — and then it didn't. Why does this happen? It's golf, I suppose."*

He also blamed a flagstick bounce in the playoff. Notice what he *didn't* mention? The three-shot lead he coughed up on Sunday. Harrington shot 67. Sergio shot 73. But sure, let's blame the flag.

Crazy, But True

One of the most popular amateur excuses is often: *"This hole hates me."*

But on one hole, it might actually be true: the 19th at Legend Golf & Safari Resort in South Africa — better known as *The Extreme 19th*. It's a **395-yard par 3**, and the tee is **437 yards above the green**. You take a helicopter just to reach it.

You'd think it's impossible to make par, let alone birdie. But 14 players have done it.

Add this one to your golf bucket list — but bring a spare dozen balls (and a pilot).

Useless Golf Trivia

Getting a hole-in-one is rare enough — **12,500-to-1** odds for amateurs. But two aces in one round? Now we're talking lottery numbers: **67 million-to-1**.

It's happened just three times in PGA Tour history. Most recently? Brian Harman at the 2015 Barclays — two aces in one round.

Then there's Patrick Willis, an amateur who drained three holes-in-one in a single round in Virginia. His playing partners were thrilled — not about the feat, but the free beers that followed.

MY SCORE DOESN'T REFLECT HOW I PLAYED   7

There's an old saying: "The front nine makes you want to quit golf. The back nine keeps you coming back."

Nobody knows this better than you.

The front nine, you're all over the place. You're in the water one hole, the woods the next. You're flubbing chips and 4-putting greens like it's your first time holding a club.

But then there's the back nine.

Suddenly you're striping balls down the fairway. You're flushing iron shots. A chip-in here, a green-in-regulation there. Never mind those three triples — you made *five* bogeys!

Then comes 18, the ultimate deceiver.

You finish with a perfect drive, reach the green in two, and two-putt for your first par of the day. It feels like a walk-off eagle.

By the time you hit the clubhouse, the front nine is erased from memory. Those triples? Forgotten. You're locked in on the back-nine magic of those bogeys and that finishing par.

- "I hit it beautifully today. The score just doesn't reflect it."
- "You shot a 104."

- "Ehhhh... I don't look at numbers. I go by feel. And I felt like a pro out there. If I start my next round like I finished this one, I'll shoot in the 60s."

Of course, next round's the same story. But you have the memory of that back-nine glory. It's enough to keep you coming back — and to cook up even more excuses about how good you *really* played.

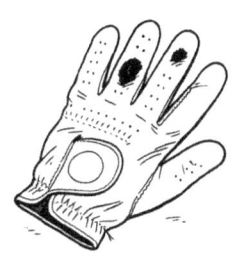

So here you go. Some of the best excuses to justify that "brilliant" 104.

"Take away the putting and I had a great round."

- **Why This is Total BS:** *That's like a pitcher saying, "Take away those six home runs and I threw a gem." Putting is part of golf. If you can't putt, you can't score.*

"In my head, I shot a much better score."

- **What It Really Means:** *You had a dream where you won the Masters. Then you woke up on the third tee with a snowman.*

"Imagine how good my score would be if I practiced."

- **What It Really Means:** *A 10-minute warm-up might've turned that 102 into a 101.*

- **How to Sell It:** *Keep groaning and stretching like you just rolled out of bed. Throw in a few neck rolls and hamstring grabs. After your first halfway decent shot, proudly declare, "See? Told you — I just needed to loosen up."*

"I just don't get this sport."

- **When to Use It:** *After your fifth chunk in a row, hands in the air like you're auditioning for a soap opera.*

"If you'd given me the right number, it would've gone in."

- **Nice Try, But No One Believes You:** You think you flushed it. You didn't. You chunked it and took a divot the size of Rhode Island.

"I made the putt. It just didn't go in."

- **Why This is Total BS:** *What is this — mini golf? Is there a clown mouth shooting the ball back? Because normally, when you make a putt, the ball goes in the hole.*

"If you gave me those 3-footers, I'd have shot in the 70s."

- **Why This Excuse Won't Fly:** *You missed 3-footers, 4-footers, and everything else.*

"I played great. The course didn't."

- **What It Really Means:** *The course beat you up and you're looking for someone to blame.*

- **How to Sell It:** *Look baffled after every shot. Mutter about the greens. Call the fairway "a disgrace." Blame the rough for being... rough.*

"Take away those doubles and I played great."

- **Why This is Total BS:** *And if you had $999,000 more, you'd be a millionaire. Still doesn't make it true.*

- **How to Sell It:** *Mid-round, sigh a lot and mutter, "Something's just off today." Then, once you're tallying up that disaster of a card, hit them with: "Honestly? I played great — if you ignore the three sixes, the two snowmans, and that 7 on the back that shouldn't even count. That hole was rigged."*

"I played great — *for someone coming off an injury.*"

- **When to Use It:** *Before the round even starts, invent an old injury — back surgery, ACL tear, maybe a phantom rotator cuff.*

- **How to Sell It:** *Limp. Groan. Stretch like you're held together with duct tape. Complain every third hole. By 18, you look like a war hero limping home — and suddenly that 106 doesn't look so bad.*

"It's so hard to shoot back-to-back great rounds."

- **When to Use It:** *On the first tee — right after you brag about that 72 last week and just before you snap-hook your drive into the trees.*

- **Nice Try, But No One Believes You:** *Sure, consistency is tough. But people who actually shoot 72 don't follow it up with a 102 and six lost balls.*

"Take that shot in the water away and it was a great round."

- **What It Really Means:** *Take away the three splashdowns, two lost in the woods, six 3-putts, and a chip that went backward... and yeah, you were lights out.*

"I'm hitting the ball well — the score just isn't showing it."

- **Why This is Total BS:** *That's like a baseball player bragging about line drives that got caught. Pretty contact, but still an out. Or in your case — still a snowman.*

"I played great once I got loose."

- **When to Use It:** *After a front nine disaster and a "less awful" back nine.*

- **How to Sell It**: *When your 8s become 6s, announce, "See? That's the real me." Too bad "real you" still lost by ten.*

"Imagine my score if we played with mulligans."

- **What It Really Means:** *With a reload every hole, you might crack 90.*

- **How to Sell It:** *Keep bragging about how pure you're hitting it. Sigh dramatically. Drop "If I could do it again..." on every tee box. By 18, you're convinced you'd shoot 68 with mulligans. Your partners are convinced you'd still break 100... barely.*

"Tee-to-green, it was the best I ever played."

- **What It Really Means:** *Don't ask about the short game.*

- **How to Sell It:** *Hype every decent drive. Flex over every green you almost hit. Ignore the four chips and three putts that followed. "Tee-to-green? I was elite." Sure, if the hole ended at 100 yards.*

"For my age, I played great."

- **When to Use It:** *Best saved for golfers north of 50. If you're using it in your 30s, prepare to get roasted.*

- **How to Sell It:** *Groan after every shot. Rub your back like you're 90. Call your partners "junior" and squint at your scorecard like it's an ancient scripture. Then finish with: "Felt like I shot my age today." Pause. "You're 97, right?"*

"I'm in great form. I'm just not scoring well."

- **When to Use It:** *When your swing looks PGA and your scorecard says mini golf.*

- **How to Sell It**: *Take 14 practice swings and pose at the top of your finish. Make slow-motion replays in real time. After every chunk, say, "Mechanically perfect, just bad luck."*

"You weren't watching any of my good shots."

- **When to Use It:** *When your group is more focused on beers than birdies.*

- **How to Sell It:** *"You didn't see that chip-in on 13?" "You were texting when I stuck it to two feet on 15!" "Where were you on 17? Hole-in-one. Swear." Bonus if you rewrite the scorecard while they're in the bathroom.*

"If only I played like I practiced."

- **What It Really Means:** *You are playing like you practiced. That's the problem.*

- **How to Sell It:** *Pretend your range session was peak Tiger. "I was hitting stingers on command. Everything was pure."*

After your fifth chunked chip, look at your wedge like it betrayed you. "This never happens on the range." Probably because you only hit the driver.

REAL SCORE JUSTIFICATION EXCUSES USED BY A PRO

We all have our favorite golfers—the ones we root for like they're family. So when they blow up in a big tournament, it feels personal. We want answers. Why did they tank the Open with a final-round meltdown? What went wrong?

We tune in, hoping to hear something concrete. Maybe there was a swing issue. Maybe it was food poisoning. Maybe a rogue yardage from the caddie.

Instead, we get this:

"I hit the ball great. My score just doesn't reflect how well I played."

Ah, yes. The oldest trick in the golfer's excuse book. Turns out, it's not just you using it. The pros have it down to a science.

Tiger Woods — 2024 U.S. Open

Tiger Woods disappointed fans with a first-round 78 at the 2024 U.S. Open.

But you know, Tiger's one of us now — because he actually *praised* the round.

> "It was probably the highest score I could have possibly shot today. I hit a lot of good shots that just didn't quite go my way."

Translation: it was also the *lowest* he could've shot.

The old Tiger would've stormed off the course, snapping clubs like Tin Cup. The new Tiger? He shrugs. He knows the end is near. Welcome to the club.

Anthony Kim — 2024 LIV Saudi Arabia

Remember Anthony Kim? He didn't vanish — he just joined LIV, which for some feels like the same thing.

After a 12-year layoff, the three-time PGA Tour winner returned with rounds in the 70s and 80s.

For most pros, that's a meltdown. Kim admitted he played like a**, but insisted it wasn't about the number.

> "I'm definitely hitting the ball well. I'm doing a lot of things well. I know the scores don't reflect that. It's disappointing to score that way."

Kim finished dead last. And has hovered near the bottom ever since. But he *feels* like he's flushing it. Sound familiar?

Crazy, But True

Some players actually *can* say, "My score doesn't reflect how well I played."

Take Arthur Thompson. At 103 years old, he shot his age at Uplands Golf Club in British Columbia.

The youngest golfer to shoot their age was Bob Hamilton, who carded a 59 at age 59.

The most strokes under age belongs to Bob Charles, who shot 66 at 76 during the 2012 Senior Open. Not bad for a guy who probably needs reading glasses to see the scorecard.

Useless Golf Trivia

You can play a flawless 17 holes — and still watch your round drown at the par-3 17th at Sawgrass.

That infamous island green has seen all kinds of carnage: an 11 from Phil Blackmar, a 12 from Bob Tway. If *they* struggle, imagine what the weekend warriors are doing.

According to course officials, about **60,000 balls** end up in the water each year. That's not a typo.

Also worth noting: you're only allowed to re-take a tee shot **twice** during a round. So after your third splash, maybe just take the drop — and your pride.

HOW TO DELIVER THE PERFECT EXCUSE

8

Okay, it's time for golf school.

Not the kind where you learn to *play* better (come on, we both know that ship sailed three drivers ago). No — this is how to *sell* a terrible round like it was just a series of freak accidents, cosmic injustice, and unfair sabotage.

Think of it like this: you're the broke guy in a tuxedo at a billionaire gala pretending you own the yacht. Confidence is everything. You have to sell it and make it believable.

The Formula:

To craft the perfect excuse, you need three things:

1. **A believable category of failure**
2. **A bit of drama (but not too much)**
3. **An absolutely straight face**

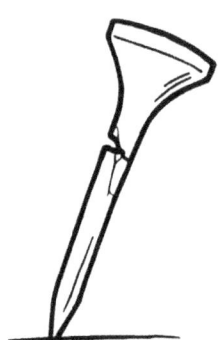

Let's start with Step 1...

Step 1: Identify the General Category of Your Failure

Which part of your game betrayed you today? Yes, it might be all of them — but pick one at a time or you'll lose credibility. Here are your main categories:

- **Driving Disasters:** *Your ball is going everywhere but forward. You're topping it, slicing it, hooking it, or just* flat-out missing it. Great if your goal was to provide a breeze on the tee box. Not so great if you want to hit the thing down the middle.

Go-to Excuses: *"The clubface is dead." "I can't swing in these shoes." "I need a stiffer shaft."*

- **Approach Tragedies:** You pull out an iron and suddenly feel like you're being audited. Every shot is chunked, bladed, or mysteriously 40 yards short. And if the shanks show up — well, may the Golf Gods help you.

  Go-to Excuses: *"I can't get a clean lie." "It's the elevation." "My clubface closed... I think."*

- **Wedge Woes:** You've got a full-blown case of the yips, and not even the strongest antibiotic can cure it. You're flubbing chips, skulling pitches, and as for bunkers? Forget it. Bring a beach chair and a piña colada — you're not getting out anytime soon.

  Go-to Excuses: *"The grass is too fluffy." "I usually love bunkers." "I caught it a little thin... or fat... or both?"*

- **Putting Problems:** Every golfer's worst nightmare. If excuses had their own encyclopedia, putting would be Volume I. You 3-putt

from 10 feet, lip out from two, and blow it five feet past trying to "make sure it got there." Whatever break you think you've read, the ball just laughs and heads the other way. Reading greens? Yeah... not exactly your superpower.

Go-to Excuses: *"These greens are unreadable." "That putt should have dropped." "The ball bobbled. Did you see that?"*

- **Mental Meltdown:**
This is when everything's against you—especially your brain. You're distracted. By everything. A bug. A breeze. The clouds. You're convinced the Golf Gods have rigged the course against you. Confidence is gone. So is any remote chance of breaking 100.

Go-to Excuses: *"The vibes are off." "I've got a lot on my mind." "I'm just out here for the walk, anyway."*

Step 2: Assign an External Factor to Take the Fall

Once you've nailed down what went wrong — sliced drive, bladed wedge, tragic 4-putt, or maybe the full disaster cocktail — it's time to level up your excuse game.

What caused it?

Whatever you do, *do not* blame yourself. That's like admitting you were wrong in an argument with your spouse. Completely unthinkable.

Instead, pick an external factor and pin it there with confidence. The truth is Irrelevant. Your job is to deflect, not reflect. Here are your all-star scapegoats, ready to take the fall:

1) The Weather

- "The wind picked up right as I swung." *(It didn't.)*

- "It's too humid to grip the club." *(Ever heard of a towel?)*

- "My hands are numb from the cold." *(It's 70°F / 21°C.)*

- "The sun's in my eyes." *(It's behind you.)*

- "It's so dry the ball's bouncing like a superball." *(You're lucky to get any roll.)*

- "I'm overheating out here." *(Also 70°F. Calm down.)*

2) The Course

- "This rough is impossible." *(It's barely overgrown lawn.)*
- "The greens are too bumpy." *(Only for you, apparently.)*
- "The tee markers are angled wrong." *(Maybe don't aim at the trees?)*

- "There's no sand in these bunkers." *(Except the mountain you just dug up.)*
- "The fairways are a mess." *(You haven't seen one all day.)*

3) The Equipment

- "These clubs aren't broken in yet." *(They're more broken-in than your car.)*
- "This driver's bent." *(It's not. But your swing is.)*
- "Still adjusting to this putter." *(You've had it for three years.)*
- "The grooves are clogged." *(Spin wasn't coming either way.)*
- "These clubs don't match my swing." *(What clubs could?)*

4) Your Body/Health

- "My back's acting up." *(So is your scorecard.)*
- "I can't focus today." *(You couldn't focus last week either.)*

- "I'm feeling under the weather." *(So is your game.)*
- "I'm just fatigued." *(That's what 14 triple bogeys will do to you.)*
- "I can't handle the pressure." *(There is no pressure — it's a friendly game.)*

5) Your Playing Partners / Other People

- "Your shadow got me." *(It's overcast.)*
- "The group behind is rushing me." *(They're still on the previous hole.)*
- "Someone yelled 'Fore' in my backswing." *(No, they yelled after you hit it at them.)*
- "That was a gimme!" *(Was it? You missed anyway.)*
- "Someone took my ball." *(Or it's in someone's garden.)*

6) The Golf Gods & Lady Luck

- "This course has it in for me." *(Join the club.)*
- "My clubs are cursed." *(Your swing is cursed.)*
- "The Golf Gods hate me." *(No argument there.)*
- "If I just got a few good bounces…" *(You'd still shoot 98.)*

Step 3: Add a Final Touch of Self-Pity

This is what separates the amateurs from the artists.

You've blamed the wind. You've cursed your clubs. You've glared at your playing partners like they ruined your childhood. Now comes the pièce de résistance — the self-pity.

The key is to *look* like a victim. Shrug. Sigh. Shake your head like your dreams just died on that last wedge shot. And deliver one of these classics with the conviction of a washed-up soap actor:

- **"This game is just unfair."**
  *Look up to the sky. Arms out.
  Wait for the heavens to reply.
  They won't.*

- **"My golf GPS is never right."**
  *Smack it against the cart
  like you're disciplining a
  disobedient toaster.*

- **"Why do I even play this stupid game?"**
  *Ask loudly enough that someone buys your next beer
  out of pity.*

- **"I'm flushing it — but the score doesn't show it."**
  *You're not. But if you say it enough times, maybe someone
  believes you. Probably not.*

- **"The wind only picks up when I swing."**
  Toss a handful of grass like you're gauging hurricane speed. Bonus if it lands in your own face.

- **"The grounds crew is out to get me."**
  Scowl at the guy mowing the green like he keyed your car.

- **"How did that putt not break?!"**
  Because it was dead straight. But blame the grain. The slope. The air pressure. Then tap your putter around like you're fixing invisible potholes.

- **"My good shots always get bad breaks."**
  Sure, and your 'good' drive was only 70 yards offline. Look shocked. Mutter something about 'bad karma.' Bonus points if you fake tearing up.

EXAMPLE EXCUSES IN ACTION

Time for your final exam. Don't worry, it's multiple choice—and like your golf game, there's no actual pressure. Just remember what you've learned: never accept blame. Ever.

Scenario 1: You yank your driver hard left into the woods. What's the best excuse to blurt out?

A) *"I turned my hips too fast on that."*

B) *"I moved my head."*

C) *"My kid must have messed with my driver. It's bent to the left. That's why I'm pulling everything."*

Correct answer: C.
Because obviously, your toddler adjusted your club's loft while building a LEGO set. Options A and B dangerously veer toward taking responsibility—don't go there. C not only blames someone else, but it adds mystery and intrigue. It's not your slice—it's sabotage.

Just be careful: if your next shot sails right, the "bent driver" narrative starts to fall apart. Time to pivot to "This shaft isn't the right flex."

Scenario 2: You 4-putt from 10 feet. What should come flying out of your mouth?

A) "I'm moving too many body parts when I putt. I need to stay more still and practice."

B) "These greens are full of leaves and spike marks. That first putt hit pollen. The next one bounced off a pebble. These greenskeepers are useless."

C) "What's wrong with me? I keep pulling my putter. I can't keep it on line."

Correct answer: B.
You can't admit to anything that sounds like a self-diagnosis. That's dangerous territory. Pretend there's a botanical garden growing on the green, even if it's Augusta. Bonus points if you pretend to inspect the green like a CSI agent, muttering "Unbelievable..." while pointing at invisible debris.

Scenario 3: You've just posted one of the worst rounds of your life. Your friends ask what went wrong.

You say:

A) "My swing was off. I need to stop scooping it and hit down more."

B) *"My putting was awful. I've tried everything. I just don't have it right now."*

C) *"I've never played this course before. At my home course I shoot in the 60s. This place doesn't suit my game. Give me two rounds and I'll be the next Scottie Scheffler."*

Correct answer: C.
Because nothing says "delusional optimism" like blaming the course you've played 37 times this year. Ignore the fact that the pro shop staff know your coffee order. Squint at the course map like you're backpacking through Slovenia. And when your friends raise an eyebrow, just double down:

"This layout's a total mismatch for my game. I need fast greens and wide fairways." (You don't. You need miracles.)

Scenario 4: Par-5. You're on the fairway. The green is 300 yards away with a group standing on it. You chunk your shot 75 yards.

What's your excuse?

A) *"I should've waited. I was worried I'd reach them and get sued. So I took a little off it. Messed with my head."*

B) *"Ugh, I picked my head up again."*

C) *"The group behind us is breathing down our necks. I rushed. I couldn't focus."*

Correct answers: A or C.
Option B is just sad. Don't go inward.

A is a bold delusion, and we respect that. Brag about your "300-yard carry" despite your driver going 160... downhill... with wind.

C is great if you want to act nervous. Fidget. Glance over your shoulder. Whisper, "They're judging me."

You won't hit it better—but you'll sound like it wasn't your fault. Mission accomplished.

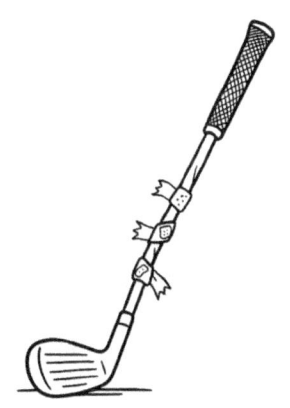

CONCLUSION: EVERY BAD SHOT IS ONE STEP CLOSER TO A GOOD ONE... RIGHT?

What is it about golf that keeps dragging us back, round after round, despite the pain? It's like gambling — except the house is the course, and you're bleeding strokes instead of chips. You lose every time, but you keep showing up. Why?

Because *hope* is a hell of a drug.

Sure, you slice it like deli meat and putt like you're using a broomstick — but hey, maybe next round you'll drive like Rory and putt like Seve. It's a one-in-ten-million shot. But you're telling me there's a chance?

That's the beauty of golf. One flushed 7-iron and suddenly your ego inflates like a hot air balloon. You cancel meetings. You skip errands. You prioritize this dumb game because *this time*, you're getting better. You can *feel* it.

And maybe you are. Kind of. But as your game improves, so do your excuses. Because the spiral is always coming. It's not *you* — it's the course. The conditions. The pairing. The 2003 shoulder injury. You can't be blamed.

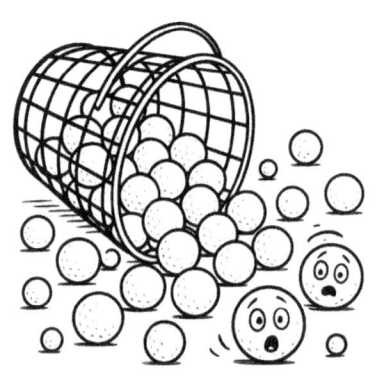

This probably already sounds like you. If it doesn't yet... just wait. You'll get there.

And when you do, we hope this book lives in your

bag — right next to the half-eaten protein bar and those 17 Top Flites waiting to be sacrificed to the nearest pond. It won't fix your game — we're not magicians — but it *will* help you sound like you know what you're doing, even if your scorecard screams otherwise.

So go out there. Post that glorious triple-digit number. Hold your head high. And convince the world none of it was your fault.

You're ready now. Go play... and blame with confidence.

BEMBERTON
BOOKS

ENJOY THE LAUGHS?

If this book gave you a chuckle, made you snort into your coffee, or reminded you of that one friend—I'd love it if you could leave a quick review or a star rating on Amazon.

(Seriously, it takes less time than lining up a three-foot putt.)

Your review helps other golfers find this book and feel slightly better about their own performance. Thanks a million!

To leave a review & help spread the word

www.ingramcontent.com/pod-product-compliance
Lightning Source LLC
Chambersburg PA
CBHW071209070526
44584CB00019B/2966